My Big Emotion Has a Name: G

Helping children understand and cope with their grief in a gentle and reassuring way.

A Note to Parents:
This book is in no way meant to replace, diagnose or treat mental illness. If you feel that your child needs help working through their big emotions, please seek professional help.

For my daughter, and the heart of gold you share with all those around you.

In a quiet town surrounded by nature, there lived a child named Mia. She had a special friend named Grief, who sometimes made her heart heavy.

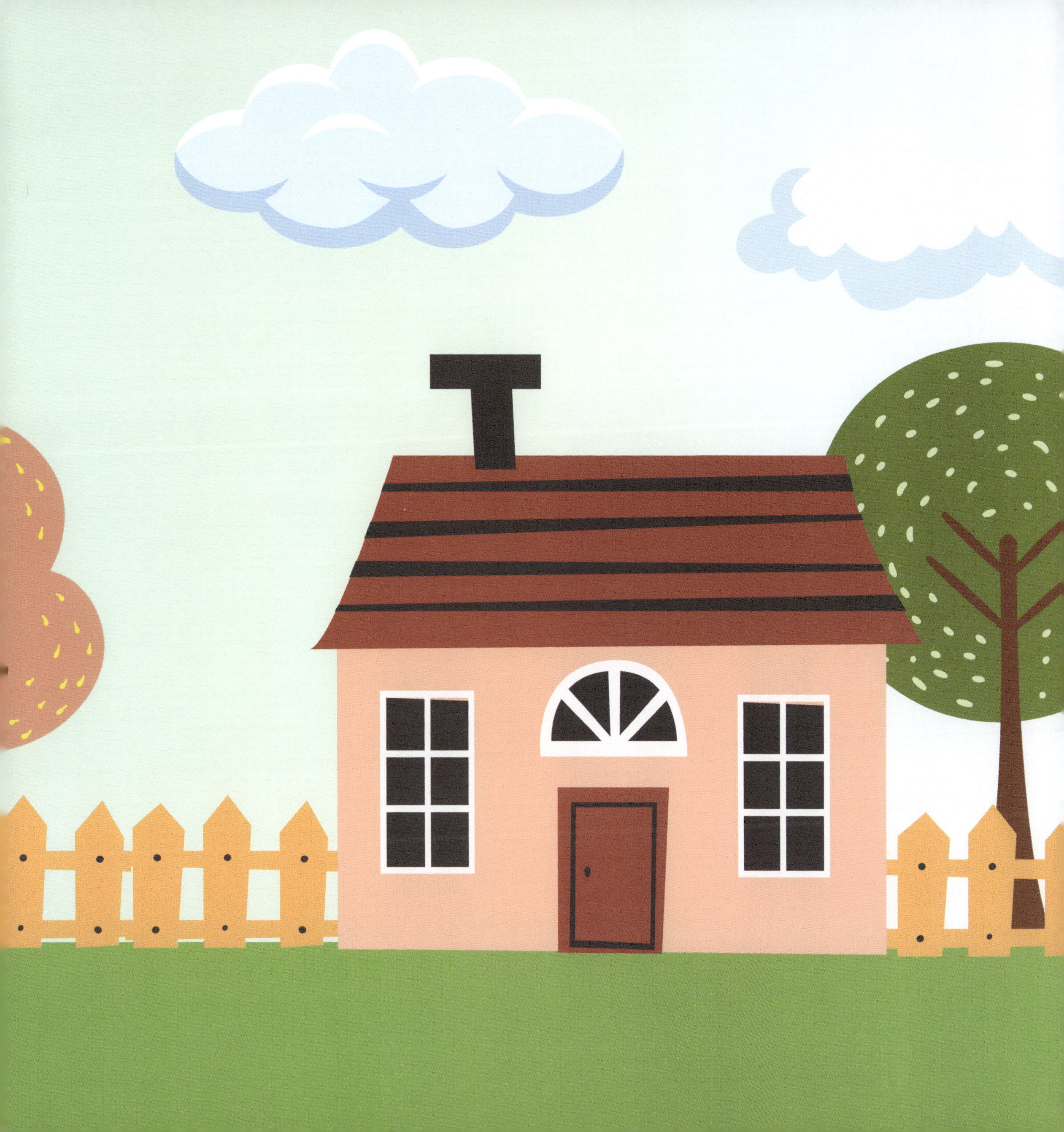

Mia knew that Grief was a quiet and shadowy friend, but sometimes, it made her feel like she was carrying a heavy burden.

Her friends were really nice, and Mia loved basketball. But when Grief came around, Mia didn't feel like playing.

One day, Mia decided it was time to learn how to cope with Grief and express those heavy feelings.

She went to her grandpa, who was kind and understanding, and said, "I want to understand my friend Grief and how to handle it."

Mia's grandpa sat Mia down next to him and explained that emotions are the body's way of telling us something, and Grief was a natural emotion, just like joy or laughter.

Mia's grandfather introduced her to a special toolbox filled with tools to help cope with Grief.

The first tool Mia's grandpa showed her was to close her eyes and take deep breaths. Mia practiced this to calm her heavy heart, breathing in for 5 seconds, holding it for 3 and then breathing out for 8 seconds.

The next tool was something Mia's grandpa called Worry Beads. Mia picked out beads of different shapes and sizes and threaded them on a little string. She could carry these in her pocket wherever she went, and when Grief came, Mia would squeeze and spin a bead, whispering the Grief out loud.

Sometimes, all Mia would have to say is "I'm okay." Other times she would say things like "my heart hurts," or "I miss my mom."

Somedays Mia would go through all her beads many times. Other days, she wouldn't have too.

The next tool was writing or drawing what Mia was feeling, and placing all these things in a Memory Box.

Mia kept the Memory Box by her bed so she could drop something in whenever she needed to.

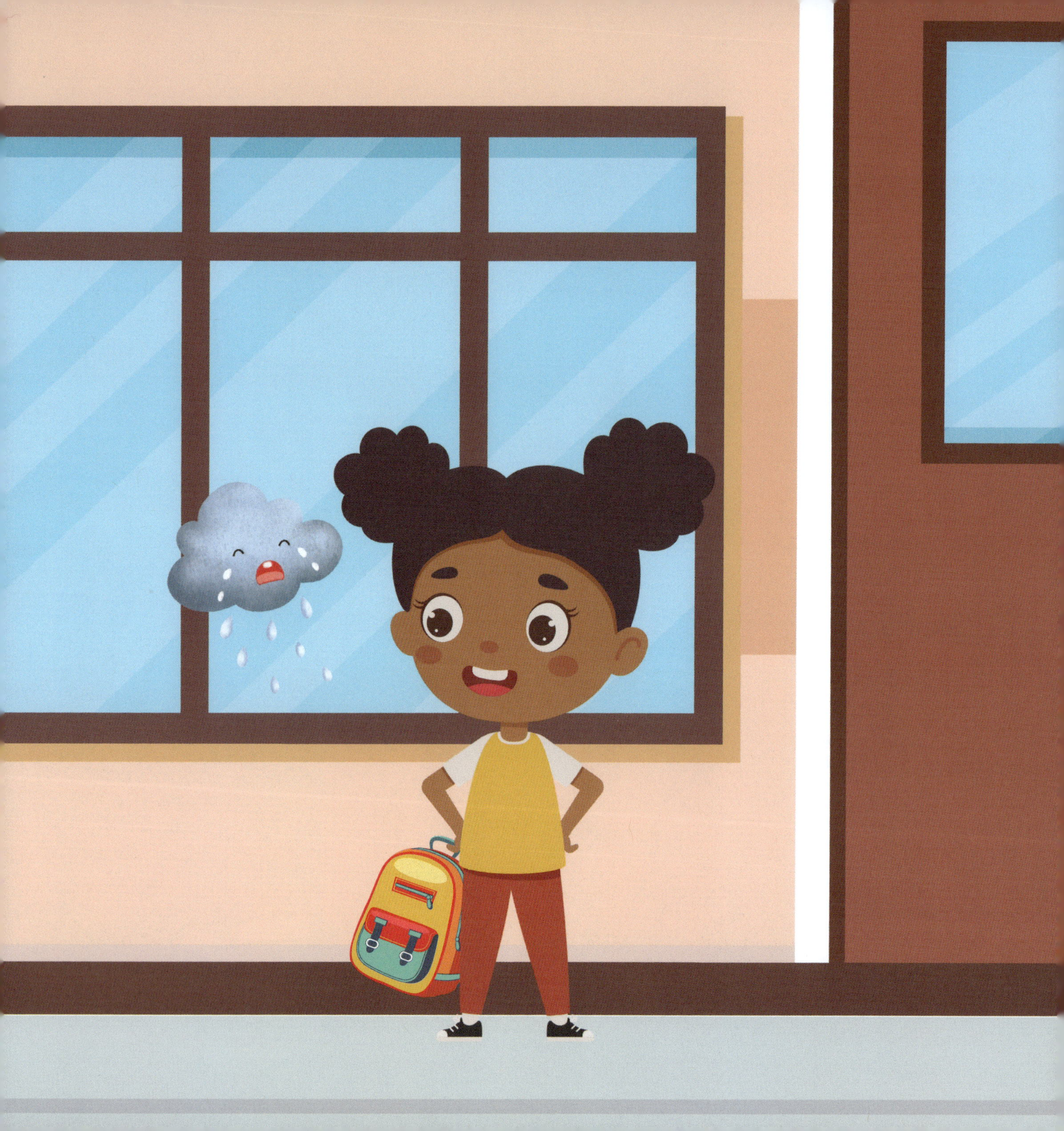

With time, Mia felt a bit lighter, even though Grief was still her friend.

She realized that even with Grief around, she could still enjoy sunny days and playful moments.

Remember, it's okay to feel grief sometimes, and with the right tools and support, you can handle it, just like Mia did.

For Parents...

Helping children cope with grief is a delicate and important process. Co-regulation, where parents provide emotional support and guidance, can be particularly beneficial during this time. Here are some tips for parents to help co-regulate their children who are experiencing grief:

Open Communication: Encourage your child to talk about their feelings and thoughts related to their grief. Create an open and non-judgmental space for them to share.

Age-Appropriate Explanations: Tailor your explanations to your child's age and level of understanding. Be honest but use language they can comprehend.

Emotional Validation: Let your child know that it's okay to feel sad, angry, or confused. Validate their emotions and reassure them that their feelings are normal.

Share Your Feelings: Express your own emotions and grief. Sharing your feelings can help your child see that it's okay to grieve and that it's a natural part of life.

Maintain Routines: Stick to daily routines as much as possible. Consistency can provide a sense of security and predictability during a challenging time.

Create a Memory Book: Encourage your child to create a memory book or scrapbook of the person or pet they have lost. This can be a healing and creative outlet for their grief.

Engage in Creative Activities: Art, music, and writing can be therapeutic. Encourage your child to express their feelings through creative outlets.

Provide Physical Comfort: Offer physical comfort through hugs, cuddles, and gentle touch. Physical closeness can be soothing during grief.

Be Patient: Grief is a process that varies for each person. Be patient and give your child the time they need to grieve in their own way.

Respect Their Choices: Allow your child to make choices about how they want to grieve, such as attending a memorial service or not.

Celebrate Memories: Share and celebrate positive memories of the person or pet they've lost. This can help focus on the joy and love that was shared.

Seek Professional Help: If your child's grief becomes overwhelming or prolonged, consider seeking the support of a child therapist or counselor who specializes in grief and loss.

Connect with Supportive People: Encourage your child to talk to friends, family members, or support groups if they feel comfortable. Sharing grief with others can be comforting.

Maintain Self-Care: As a parent, remember to take care of yourself. You need to be emotionally healthy to support your child through their grief.

Remember that everyone processes grief differently, and it's essential to provide a loving and understanding environment for your child during this challenging time. Your presence and support are invaluable in helping them navigate their grief.

Printed in Great Britain
by Amazon